RUBA'IYAT OF RUMI

Sufi Pocketbook Series

For a complete list of our publications

go to amazon.com/author/smithpa

RUBA'IYAT OF RUMI

Sufi Pocketbook Series

Translation & Introduction

Paul Smith

NEW HUMANITY BOOKS

Book Heaven

Booksellers & Publishers

NEW HUMANITY BOOKS

BOOK HEAVEN

(Booksellers & Publishers for over 50 years)

47 Main Road Campbells Creek Victoria 3451

Australia

ISBN: 9798665617466

Poetry/Mysticism/Sufism/Persian Literature/
Middle Eastern Studies

CONTENTS

Life & Times & Poetry of Rumi

Jalal-ud-din Rumi was born in 1207 in Balkh. This city was then in the Persian province of Khorasan but is now in Afghanistan. Balkh was a prominent city at that time and his family had a tradition of service there in both legal and religious offices. Despite this he moved when about eleven with his family away from Balkh so as to avoid the warlike Mongols. They travelled to Baghdad, to Mecca on pilgrimage, to Damascus and eventually settled near Konya, Turkey.

On the road to Anatolia, Jalal-ud-din and his father had encountered one of the most famous mystic Persian poets, Farid ad-din Attar, in the city of Nishapur. Attar immediately recognised the boy's spiritual status. He saw Baha-ud-din, walking ahead of his son and said, "Here comes a sea followed by an ocean." He gave Jalal-ud-din his *Illahi-nama,* 'Book of God'. This meeting had a deep impact on Rumi's thoughts, which became the inspiration for his masterpiece *Masnavi.*

Baha-ud-din became the head of a *madrassa* (religious college) and when he died Rumi succeeded him at the age of twenty-five. He married and had two sons. One of Baha-ud-din's students, Syed Burhan-ud-din, continued to train Rumi in the religious and mystical doctrines of Rumi's father. For nine years, Rumi practiced Sufism as a disciple of Burhan-ud-din until Burhan-ud-din died in 1240. During this period Rumi travelled to Damascus and is said to have spent four years there. While there he first caught a glimpse of the *Qutub* (Perfect Master) Shams-e Tabriz clothed in his black-felt cap. Shams called out to him but he turned away and mixed in with the crowd in the market. On returning to Konya Rumi fasted for three consecutive periods of forty days under the guidance of Burhan-ud-din. He pronounced that he had taught Rumi all he could of all sciences, human and spiritual.

In 1244 the perfected dervish Shams-e Tabriz arrived in Konya. This great Spiritual Master, a basket-maker by trade had travelled much in search of other great souls. He went to an inn in Konya under the disguise of a merchant where he began fasting on and off. One day as he sat near the inn's gate Rumi rode up on a mule followed by a large crowd of his many students and disciples on foot. Shams stood then walked over to him and took hold of the mule's bridle and halted the animal and after paying due reverence to the great teacher asked Rumi the following question, "Was Mohammed the greater servant of God, or Bayzid of Bistam?"

Rumi answered, "Incomparably, Mohammed was the greater... the greatest of all the prophets and saints!"

Shams then asked, "Why is it then that Mohammed said, 'We haven't known You God as You should rightly be known' while Bayzid declared, 'Glory be to me! How very great is my glory!'?"

With this Shams had revealed his state of being *Qutub* or Perfect Master to Rumi.

Rumi fainted. On recovering consciousness he asked Shams to come home with him where they were closeted together for weeks and then months and then years in spiritual communication. Four years later on the night of the fifth of December 1248, as Rumi and Shams were talking, Shams was called to the back door. He went out, never to be seen again. It is believed that he was murdered with the help of one of Rumi's sons, Allaedin... Rumi's students and followers had become frustrated and jealous with Shams taking up all the time of their teacher.

Rumi's love and his great longing for Shams, whom he went searching for in Damascus and elsewhere, found expression in music, dance, songs and poems in his collection of poems/songs or *Divan* which he named after his Master... *Divan of Shams-e Tabriz*. This vast work included thousands of *ghazals* and other poetic forms and nearly two thousand *ruba'is* which he would compose for many years, before he became a God-realised Perfect Master himself, and also afterwards.

Ruba'i: Its Form, Function & History

Most scholars of Persian Poetry agree that the *ruba'i* is the most ancient Persian poetic form that is original to this language. All other classical forms including the *ghazal, qasida, masnavi* etc., they say originated in Arabic literature and the metres employed in them were in Arabic poetry in the beginning. The *ruba'i* is a poem of four lines in which usually the first, second and fourth lines rhyme and sometimes with the *radif* (refrain) after the rhyme words... sometimes all four rhyme. It is composed in metres called *'ruba'i'* metres. Each *ruba'i* is a separate poem in itself and should not be regarded as a part of a long poem as was created by FitzGerald when he translated those he attributed to Omar Khayyam.

The *ruba'i* (as its name implies) is two couplets *(beyts)* in length, or four lines *(misra)* as stated above. The *ruba'i* is different in metre from all those used in Arabic poetry that preceded it. How was this metre invented? The accepted story of Rudaki (d. 941 A.D.) creating this new *metre* of the *hazaj* group which is essential to the *ruba'i* is as follows: one New Year's Festival he happened to be strolling in a garden where some children played with nuts and one threw a walnut along a groove in a stick and it jumped out then rolled back again creating a sound and the children shouted with delight in imitation, *'Ghaltan ghaltan hami ravad ta bun-i gau,'* (*Ball, ball, surprising hills... to end of a brave try*). Rudaki immediately recognised in the line's metre a new invention and by the repetition four times of the *rhyme* he had quickly created the *ruba'i...* and is considered the first master of this form and the father of classical Persian Poetry.

Shams-e Qais writing two hundred years later about this moment of poetic history and the effect of this new form on the population said the following... "This new poetic form fascinated all classes, rich and poor, ascetic and drunken outsider/*rend*/, all wanted to participate in it... the sinful and the good both loved it; those who were so ignorant they couldn't make out the difference between poetry and prose began to dance to it; those with dead hearts who couldn't tell the difference between a donkey braying and reed's wailing and were a thousand miles away from listening to a lute's strumming, offered up their souls for a *ruba'i*. Many a young girl cloistered away, out of passion for the song of a *ruba'i* broke down the doors and their chastity's walls; many matrons from love for a *ruba'i* let loose the braids of their self-restraint."

The *ruba'i* should be eloquent, spontaneous and ingenious. In the *ruba'i* the first three lines serve as an introduction to the fourth that should be sublime, subtle or pithy and clever. As can be seen from the quote by Shams-e Qais above the *ruba'i* immediately appealed to all levels of society and has done so ever since. The nobility and royalty enjoyed those in praise of them and the commoner enjoyed the short, simple homilies... the ascetic and mystic could think upon epigrams of deep religious fervour and wisdom; the reprobates enjoyed the subtle and amusing satires and obscenities... and for everyone, especially the cloistered girls and old maids, many erotic and beautiful love poems to satisfy any passionate heart.

Every major and most minor poet of Persia composed at some times in the *ruba'i* form. I will now attempt a short history of the finest exponents and innovators of this form up to Rumi (1208-1274)... many of course would have had an influence on him, (then a brief look at

15

what Rumi brought to this form)... until about two hundred years after him... ending with Jami (1414-1493) and the end of Persian Classical Literature. A fuller exploration of this subject, with a much greater selection of poems and sources can be discovered in my *The Ruba'iyat: A World Anthology* (see bibliography).

*

RUDAKI was born in the village of Rudak (hence his pen-name or *takhallus*) in Transoxania in 858 A.D. The historian 'Awfi says that Rudaki was blind from birth but other historians of the time disagree with him asking how one could create such images of nature if he did not at one time see. Others say that a ruler later in his life held red-hot iron rods before his eyes and blinded him when he refused to compose poetry for him.

First a wandering 'dervish' poet he later served at the court of the Samanids of Bokhara. Rudaki was so intelligent and like Hafiz of Shiraz (1320-1392) blessed with such a fine memory that by the age of eight he had memorised all of the *Koran.* He is said to have had a happy childhood spending much of his time listening to stories and songs and learning about his people's ways and aspirations. He began to compose poems expressing their desires and his own. He had a beautiful voice and was a fine musician and because of this he mixed freely with other minstrels and with musicians and dancers. His lute teacher was the famous Bakhtiar and he eventually excelled his master. He travelled around the Tajikistan highlands with his master, singing and creating songs. When Bakhtiar died and left him his famous lute he continued wandering and singing until his fame reached the capital... Bokhara.

Nasr ibn Ahmad summoned him to his court and he prospered there amassing great wealth. He had 200 slaves in his retinue... and 400 camels carried his belongings when he travelled. He was commissioned and paid 40,000 *dirhams* to translate *Kalila and Dimna* (a collection of fables originating in India and translated into Arabic in 750) into Persian verse *(masnavi...* rhyming couplets). This work, plus most of the reported 1,300,000 couplets (some say 130,000) that he composed (his *Divan*) have not survived the ravages of time. There remain only 1000 couplets... 52 *kasidas, ghazals* and *ruba'is.* Of his epic masterpieces we have nothing beyond a few lines. In 937 he fell out of favour at court (perhaps he was blinded at this time) after the death of the prime-minister who had supported him. His life ended in abject poverty, forgotten by the world at that time. Rudaki died in Rudak in 941. His poetry is about the passage of time, old age, death, fortune's fickleness, importance of the matters of the heart, the need to be happy. Although he praised kings, nobles and heroes... his greatest love was knowledge and experience.

With what one has, be satisfied,
live freely:
by any formality do not be tied...
live freely!
Don't pity self if others seem richer:
many more are by fortune tried.
Live, freely!

*

BABA TAHIR ('The Naked')... d.1020, was a great God-intoxicated soul (*mast*) and possibly a *Qutub* (Perfect Master) who composed about 60 known *ruba'i* in a simpler metre than the usual *'hazaj'* metre. His simple, mystical poems that he would sing while wandering naked throughout the land had a profound influence on Sufis and dervishes and other *ruba'i* composers that followed him, especially Abu Said.

> *I am a kalandar… a drunken outsider, a*
> *vagabond,*
> *on such a one like me life has no ties, no*
> *bond:*
> *during day I wander aimlessly… at night*
> *my pillow's a stone… my lamp the moon*
> *beyond.*

*

FIRDAUSI (941- 1021). Next, in our tracing of the *ruba'i* through the words of Persia's greatest exponents of the poetic arts, we come to Iran's national poet, known throughout the land and many others as the creator of the 60,000 couplets he called 'Book of Kings' or *Shah-nama*. He was a lot less prolific than Iran's previous other 'immortal', Rudaki, and occasionally gave up the *masnavi* form of different rhyming couplets and composed in the *ruba'i* form. Born the year that Rudaki died, in Tus, the ancient city in Khorasan, Abdul Qasim Mansur would use the *takhallus* or pen-name of Firdousi (Paradise) calling himself that after the name of a garden his father looked after... being a small but proud landowner. His *Shah-nama* took thirty years to complete and he was only paid 20,000 *dirhams* of the 50,000 promised to him by Sultan Mahmud and he bitterly wrote satires on that ruler in his old age. The following *ruba'i* was possibly composed about the Sultan in earlier, happier times...

Showing his servants much kindness
last night,

he acted like a human being, no less,
last night.
Faults forgiving, taking arm, laughing
loudly, it... around his neck he did press
last night.

*

ABU SAID (948-1049) was the famous Perfect
Master who composed over 400 *ruba'is*. He is
considered to be the founder of Sufi poetry and
was a major influence on the *ruba'i* and most
poets that followed. especially Sana'i, Attar and
Rumi.

This body was all tears that were by my eyes
shed,
in this love for You one must have no form or
head.

What is this love? Not one trace of me stays!
Who is the lover, ever since I've become... the
Beloved?

*

IBN SINA (981-1037). Abu 'Ali Ibn Sina (or as he is called in the west... Avicenna) born some forty years after Firdousi in Bukhara died about twenty-five years after him, living only for fifty-six years even though he was one of the greatest creative exponents of the great arts of *Koranic* knowledge, arithmetic and algebra, medicine, surgery and philosophy and wrote poems in Arabic and Persian so much so that that some *ruba'is* he composed were later to be ascribed to Omar Khayyam. He was hounded as a heretic and worse, but all the known world is still trying to catch up to what he discovered. His *kasida* on the human soul is considered one of the greatest

Persian poems of all time. His *ruba'is* are some of the most honest and direct of all time.

I was asked by a person, "Tell me, what is
the Absolute?"
Beyond description and imaginable bliss…
the Absolute!
One cannot speak of why It is or what It is:
only the Absolute can really say, "This… is
the Absolute!"

*

BABA KUHI… d.1051. A Perfect Master poet who lived in the fabled city of Shiraz. His tomb is on a hill outside that city and it was at that tomb that the greatest of all Persian mystical love poets Hafiz kept vigil for forty nights and received from this Master the gift of poetry, immortality and 'his heart's delight'.

Ever since the First Day as drunken lover
I've come
with the winecup in hand... until forever,
I've come.
I am lover, drunkard, worshipper of wine:
do not blame me for like this I was before
I've come.

*

ANSARI (1006-1089). The great mystical poet Khwaja Abdullah Ansari who passed from this world 1089 in Herat is most known for his biographical dictionary on saints and masters and his much loved collection of inspiring prayers, the *Munajat*. His *ruba'is* appear throughout his works.

From loving you, without soul and heart

I've become,

twisted like your curls, that play a part,

I've become.

No, a mistake: now that by love's power

I'm beyond both worlds, the Sweetheart

I've become.

*

AL-GHAZZALI (1058-1112). Mohammad al-Ghazzali the famous theologian was born in Tus in 1058 and after his many extraordinary expositions on the knowledge of the spiritual path, Islamic philosophy was never the same. He has been called 'The Proof of Islam' and the learned Suyuti once said of him, "If there could have been another prophet after Mohammed it would surely have been al-Ghazzali!" His *Alchemy of Happiness* is of course his most popular work but he was also a composer of a number of fine *ruba'is*.

> *O Being's Essence... is there one being*
> *You are not in?*
> *You are no place, but there is no thing...*
> *You are not in?*
> *O You, not needing direction or place...*
> *what, is Your Place? Is a place missing,*
> *You are not in?*

*

OMAR KHAYYAM (died 1132). Of the 1000 or so *ruba'is* attributed to him only about ten percent are now considered to be his. More famous in Iran as an astronomer and mathematician his nihilistic and hedonistic philosophy in his *ruba'is* meant that his poems were never really popular in his homeland.

Don't let your soul in sorrow's grasp be

pressed,

don't let your days be filled... with vain

unrest:

book, beloved's lips, meadow's edge don't

give up... even if the earth folds you in its

breast.

*

SANA'I (d. 1131). One of the most prolific and influential Sufi Master Poets of all time Sana'i composed many *ghazals, masnavis* and over 400 *ruba'is*. His long *masnavi* (rhyming couplets) mystical work *The Enclosed Garden of the Truth* is said to have had a profound influence on Rumi's composing his *Masnavi* and Sadi's his *Bustan* ('The Orchard').

Go to the winehouse, be a drunken lover
only:
there, wine and music and beloved order,
only.
Fill the large cup and before flagon of wine
joyfully drink... speak sense to him or her
only.

*

MAHSATI (1098-1185). We know little of
Mahsati Ganjavi's life except that she lived in
Ganjeh where Sultan Sanjar reigned and as she
was a poet at his court she would have known
Anvari. She was a court, dervish and ribald poet.
She knew Nizami (she is said to have been
buried in his mausoleum) and Omar Khayyam...
and like Omar composed only in the *ruba'i* form
and must be considered not only a master of that
form but also to have helped revolutionise it. She
was an influence on perhaps Iran's greatest

female poet Jahan Khatun of Shiraz and Iran's greatest satirist Obeyd Zakani. She was famous and also infamous for her liberated behaviour and is said to have had many affairs not only with the sultan who found her of interest when after he was about to mount his horse discovered a sudden fall of snow had covered the field and she composed for him the following *ruba'i* on the spot...

For you... Heaven has saddled Fortune's
steed
O sultan... and chosen you from all who
lead:
it spreads a silver sheet on the ground,
steed's gold-shod hooves... mud won't
impede.

*

ANVARI (d. 1187). A court poet of the Seljik sultans. Jami composed a *ruba'i* where he names him along with Firdausi and Sadi as one of the 'three apostles' of Persian poetry. Mainly a court poet he was also an astrologer.

I spent many a night until morning wanting
you...
many happy days kissing your lips I had, it's
true:
now that you have gone, day and night I say,
"Day I meet beloved, let that night be happy
too!"

*

NIZAMI (d. 1208). Another Master Poet who is most famous for his six books in *masnavi* form: *The Treasury of the Mysteries, Layla and Majnun, Khrosrau and Shirin, The Seven*

Portraits and his two books on Alexander. He also composed a *Divan* of approximately 20,000 couplets in *ghazals* and *ruba'is*... tragically only 200 couplets survive. His influence on Attar, Rumi, Sadi, Hafiz and Jami and all others that followed was profound.

"May my words with you have value,"
I said,
"Patience in love God give to me too,"
I said.
You... "Why do you pray?" "Union!"
You replied, "May God give it to you,
I said."

*

RUZBIHAN... d. 1210. This Sufi Perfect Master of Shiraz is better known for his Spiritual Diary... *The Unveiling of Secrets*. He wrote mainly in Arabic and his *rubai's* are few of his works in Persian.

Searching for the cup of Jamshid the world I travelled:
I didn't rest a day... sleep never entered my head.
When Jamshid's cup I heard by my Master described,
that I myself was that world-seeing cup... I realised.

*

'ATTAR (d. 1230). Farid ad-din 'Attar is the Perfect Master Poet who was the author of over forty books of poetry and prose including *The Conference of the Birds, The Book of God* (which as previously stated he is said to have presented to Rumi when he met him) and *The*

Lives of the Saints. Apart from his many books in *masnavi* form he also composed many hundreds of mystical *ghazals* and *ruba'is.* He also changed the evolution of the *ruba'i* form by composing a long Sufi epic, the *Mukhtar-nama,* where each *ruba'i* is connected to the one before, something which Fitzgerald attempted to do with those he attributed to Omar Khayyam.

Heart, since you drank spiritual knowledge's
wine,
keep lips closed… don't sell any secrets of the
Divine.
Don't boil like mountain spring in difficulties:
if you sit, silently, You will become Ocean, so
fine.

*

SADI (1210-1291). Sadi of Shiraz, a contemporary of Rumi who influenced him, was another Master Poet who expressed himself in the *ruba'i* form as well as hundreds of *ghazals* in his beautiful *Divan* that often also contained images from dervish dancing. Sadi was a great traveller who spent forty years on the road throughout the Middle-East, North Africa and India and many of the incidents he experienced he wrote down in his two most famous works when he finally returned to his beloved birth-place... The Rose Garden *(Gulistan)* and The Orchard *(Bustan)*.

Than anything else, to cure another's suffering
is better:
more, not less... other people one to be helping
is better.
Friend, in hands of my enemies don't leave me:
if I am to be dying, Your hand to me be killing,
is better.

KHAJU KERMANI (1281-1352). Born in Kerman he was the court poet in Baghdad then Yazd and eventually in Shiraz and knew Hafiz, Obeyd Zakani and Jahan Malek Khatun. He was accused of plagiarising the work of Sadi and was the author of five *masnavi* epics and hundreds of court and Sufi *ghazals* and *ruba'is*. His tomb is in Shiraz.

Our ecstasy and listening is no mere
fancy,
and this dance we do is not a game to
see:
say to the unknowing, "Ignorant ones,
any nonsense so drawn out would not
be!"

*

OBEYD ZAKANI (1300-1371) Persia's greatest satirist and social commentator of the classical period (some say of all time) he was most likely a teacher and friend of Hafiz and a strong influence upon him and a lover of Jahan Khatun (to follow). After moving from the court at Baghdad he spent many years in Shiraz as a court poet and court jester. His masterpiece epic poem *Cat and Mouse* is still fresh and his ribald and outright obscene stories and *ruba'is* are still frowned upon by authorities in Iran. His mystical *ghazals* and *ruba'is* are now considered to be some of the most profound and revolutionary for the period. He was exiled from Shiraz for as a result of his criticism of the dictator Mubariz.

I said... "The glorious face of God... is your face."

Answer: "True... straight as my form full of
grace!"
I said: "On your arse is no hair... not even a
trace!"
You: "Such kindness, your describing of that
place."

*

HAFIZ (1320-1392). Persia's greatest exponent of the *ghazal* Hafiz became a Perfect Master *(Qutub)*, was twice exiled from his beloved Shiraz for his criticism of rulers and false Sufi masters and hypocritical clergy. His *Divan* shows he composed in other forms including the *masnavi* and the *ruba'i* of which about 150 have come down to us. As with his *ghazals*, his *ruba'is* are sometimes mystical and sometimes critical of the hypocrisy of his times.

Your soul's completely covered me in deepest

ecstasy;

I desired You, but grief was holding my heart

tightly...

if, I am unable to find You in place one prays,

in the Winehouse of Love, Your lips... are my

discovery.

*

JAHAN KHATUN (1326-1416?) Daughter of
the king of one of Shiraz's most turbulent
times... Masud Shah; pupil and lifelong friend of
the world's greatest mystical, lyric poet, Hafiz of
Shiraz; the object of crazed desire by (among
others) Iran's greatest satirist, the obscene,
outrageous, visionary poet Obeyd Zakani; lover,
then wife of womaniser Amin al-Din, a minister
of one of Persia's most loved, debauched and
tragic rulers... Abu Ishak; cruelly imprisoned for

twenty years under the Muzaffarids while her young daughter mysteriously died; open-minded and scandalous, one of Iran's first feminists... the beautiful and sensuous, petite princess who abdicated her royalty twice; one of Iran's greatest classical lyric poets whose *Divan* is four times larger than that of Hafiz's and contains about 2000 *ghazals* and hundreds of *ruba'is.*

I swore that him again I would never see:
deaf to temptations of sin... I'd be a Sufi!
Then I knew it wasn't in my nature...
renunciations are now renounced, by me!

*

JAMI (1414-1493). Considered the last great poet of the Classical Period (10th-15thC.) Jami is most known for his masterpiece seven *masnavis* epics… including *Joseph and Zulaikh, Layla and Majnun,* and *Salman and Absal.* He also composed three *Divans* consisting of *ghazals rubai's* and other mystical poems.

For this worn out world, each day suffering,
I did go:
for what is and is not, each night… desiring,
I did go!
Each moment of life that seemed like a world,
to say it simply… futile thoughts… thinking,
I did go.

From the above examples it can be seen that the *ruba'i* was used to communicate a wide variety of subjects from the most mystical to the satirical and even the obscene. Even today this form is used in Iran and elsewhere to express an unlimited number of feelings and subjects.

SELECTED BIBLIOGRAPHY

Divan of Rumi: Translation & Introduction by Paul Smith. New Humanity Books 2016.

The Ruba'iyat of Jalal al-din Rumi: Selected translations into English Verse by A.J. Arberry. Emery Walker, Ltd. London 1949.

The Quatrains of Rumi, Translated by Ibrahim W. Gamard and A.G. Rawan Farhadi: Complete Translation with Persian Text, Islamic Mystical Commentary, Manual of Terms, and Concordance. Sufi Dari Books, San Rafael, 2008. (Literal trans. of all 1852 of Rumi's ruba'is).

The Mathnawi of Jalalu'ddin Rumi Edited from the oldest manuscripts available: with critical notes, translation, & commentary by Reynold A. Nicholson 8 vols. Luzac & Co. London 1926. (The recognized literal trans., but has recently come under much criticism by good scholars for his excluding many true couplets and his mistranslation of key words.)

The Masnavi: Jalal al-din-Rumi, Books One & Two Translated with an Introduction & notes by Jawid Mojaddedi, Oxford University Press, 2004. (A wonderful Trans. of the 1ˢᵗ two books in the correct ryme... more to come I hope).

Rumi: Selected Poems, Translation and Introduction by Paul Smith, New Humanity Books Campbells Creek, 2012.

Maulana Rumi's Masnawi Translation and commentary by M.G. Gupta. 6 vols. MG Publishers Agra. 1990.

The Mesnevi of Mevlana (Our Lord) Jelal-ud-din, Muhammad, Er-Rumi. Book the First: Together with some account of The Life and Acts of the Author, of his Ancestors, and of his descendants, by Mevlana Shems-ud-din Ahmed, El Eflaki, El Arifi Translated, and Poetry Versified by James W. Redhouse. Trubner & Co. London 1881

Mystical Poems of Rumi... First Selection, Poems 1-200. Translated from the Persian by A.J. Arberry The University of Chicago Press. 1968. (200 of his ghazals in literal trans.).

Mystical Poems of Rumi... Second Selection, Poems 201-400. Translated by A.J. Arberry. Westview Press, Boulder Colorado. 1979. (200 more of his many ghazals in literal trans.)

Divan-i Kebir: Mevlana Celaleddin Rumi. Translated by Nevit O. Ergin from the Turkish translations. Echo Publications, California 22 vols. 1995-2003. (All of his ghazals in literal trans. from trans. into Turkish!)

Discourses of Rumi... Translated by A.J. Arberry. John Murray, London. 1961.

Rumi. Past and Present, East and West. The Life, Teaching and Poetry of Jalal al-Din Rumi. Franklin D. Lewis Oneworld Publications Oxford 2000.

I Am Wind You Are Fire: The Life and Work of Rumi. Annemarie Schimmel Shambhala Publications Boston. 1992

A Thousand Years of Persian Ruba'iyat. An Anthology of Quatrains from the Tenth to the Twentieth Century Along with the Original Persian. Translated into English by Reza Saberi. Ibex Pub., Bethesda, Maryland. 2000. (pp. 222-262).

Piercing Pearls: The Anthology of Persian Poetry. Sufi, Dervish, Court, Satirical, Ribald and Prison Poetry from the 9th-20th C. Translations, Introduction by Paul Smith. New Humanity Books 2012. (Includes a selection Rumi's ruba'is and ghazals and masnavis and a large selection of other poems of other Persian Poets he influenced and who influenced him.)

A Literary History of Persia by Edward B. Browne Volume 2. Cambridge University Press. Reprint 1969.

The Ilahi-nama or Book of God of Farid al-Din 'Attar Translated from the Persian by John Andrew Boyle. Manchester U. Press, 1976. (For Mahsati see pages 218-220).

Obeyd Zakani: The Dervish Fool. A Selection of His Poetry, Prose, Satire, Jokes & Ribaldry. Transation & Introduction by Paul Smith. New Humanity Books 2010.

Hafiz's Friend, Jahan Khatun: Persia's Princess Dervish Poet. A Selection of Poems from Her Divan. Translation Paul Smith, Rezvaneh Pashai. New Humanity Books 2006, 2010.

History of Iranian Literature. Jan Rypka and others. D. Reidel Publishing Company. 1968.

The Shahnama of Firdausi. 8 vols. Translated by Arthur George Warner and Edmond Warner. Kegan Paul, Trench, Trubner & Co. Ltd. 1923. (Available in Adobe Acrobat format from saladin20@yahoo.com)

Layla & Majnun by Nizami. Translation and Introduction by Paul Smith. New Humanity Books 2007.

The Treasury of the Mysteries by Nizami. Translation and Introduction by Paul Smith. New Humanity Books 2005.

Divan of Sadi. His Mystical Love Poetry. Translation & Introduction by Paul Smith. New Humanity Books 2006.

The Ruba'iyat: A World Anthology. Translations & Introduction by Paul Smith, New Humanity Books Campbells Creek 2009.

The Sufi & Dervish Ruba'iyat Translations & Introduction by Paul Smith, New Humanity Books, Campbells Creek, 2009.

Ruba'iyat of Rumi

What is inside and out, and what is vice and

virtue

by command of God is, and is destined to be,

too.

I continue to keep trying, but Destiny says...

"It's beyond you, there's a Power greater than

you!"

To be lover and dervish* at the same time is

kingly…

sorrow of love is a treasure that one cannot

see:

with my hands the heart's treasure I ruined

completely…

I knew in ruins, treasure would be found, by

me.

Than impatient lover, is there a more miserable

person?

Such a love as this, is a dilemma... that has no

solution:

remedy for love's pain is not patience, nor bold

assertion...

in love that is true, there's no faith, no cruelty:

none!

I went over to see the doctor, and I asked him

this:

"What do you advise one... who fallen in love

is?"

He said... "Give up *you,* obliterate your own

existence:

I'm saying to leave all existence, this... is my

analysis!"

O You, who could be likened to the only sun...

come!

Without Your face, flowers pale in any garden:

come!

Without You, this world is mere dust... ashen,

come!

Without You, this joyful gathering is frozen...

come!

When I'm with You… from loving,

I can't sleep:

when I'm not with You, from crying

I can't sleep.

O God, both nights I'm wide awake!

It differs? When in bed, I am lying…

I can't sleep!

Upon the pathway of calamity

I laid my heart

down... only for You, to see...

I laid my heart!

Breeze brought Your scent here,

and down to breeze, thankfully,

I laid my heart.

But for love, there wasn't a companion

for me:

no other beginning, at first, or later on,

for me.

Inside me I can hear the soul calling me:

"Lazy one on love's road... do not go on

for me."

Cleverly, I should my self be throwing…

there,

to see if that Soul of the world is waiting

there.

That Ideal I desire, I will keep walking to:

or, like this heart, I'll my head be losing…

there.

Because of wine… this head is full of
confusion:
Your lips of sugar add sweetness, in
profusion.
*Winebringer, as You gave many cups,
it's true all secrets will be told… later
on.

Drunk, notorious all year round may the lover

be:

in a frenzy, spellbound and crazy, let him be...

constantly.

When sober we suffer, because of everything,

but when so intoxicated... everything we set

free.

Your rose-garden, I have not seen…

for a long time:

Your drunken eyes, away have been,

for a long time.

Like faithfulness You're far from all:

Your beautiful face I have not seen…

for a long time.

For as long as I live my faith to *Koran* of God

I give:

Chosen One, Mohammed, is Lord, for as long as

I live…

if anyone thought I've written anything but this

I don't care a fig about that one, or whatever his

perspective.

Again, O Majesty, accept the service I
bring...
upon my grief and weakness, mercy be
showing.
O Lord, if ever against Your Word I am
going,
do not help me again if out of pain I am
calling.

When You made me to go walking along faith's

way...

to be true until death, Your trust on me You did

lay.

I cried... "I feel faint and my burden's so great:"

You, then gave me the strength, to let it on me,

stay.

Quickly to an end time takes the way most men

go:

wolf of death, makes such stupid sheep's blood,

flow.

See how, with heads held high, so proudly they

go...

until Fate knocks them down dead... a sudden

blow!

Seek justice and then confess, for in Love is

righteousness;

in yourself lies the fault, as you are prone to

sinfulness.

If you don't make claim to Love's holy Name

then... prove it is a long way from Love, to...

lustfulness.

You and your soul are entwined you've but two

days:

to say a word of death to you, is an impossibility,

always.

Soul seeks a home, death is the only home ahead,

but in the middle of the road's your ass: it, asleep

stays.

One whose soul's confused is happy with yes or

no,

his difficulty with Being and Non-being... does

show.

How can one be stopped by an action, or effect,

who is of the creation free, and is the Creator...

also?

In that lane of your imagination, why do you

grope…

vainly bathing your eyes in the blood of… no

hope?

Head to foot in reality you know the Truth…

O blind heart, what illusion do you seek, you

dope?

O you, who a Country beyond any skies

do have...

the misconception your life in dust lies...

do have.

Your image of self on earth you painted,

forgetting you, birth-Place beyond size,

do have.

You are searching the earth for your great
unwinding...
your birth was in union, parting is in your
dying.
You are lying, sleeping... beside the river,
thirsting;
cursed, near the treasure... dying, while...
begging!

Union does not lie this way as you wrongly

thought,

it's in soul's world that goal you forgot, and

fought.

That river of Everlasting Life, which Khizer *

sought,

is where you are now... but, you stopped its

onslaught.

That thief, the moon, last night came down to

me…

I said, "Go, tonight this is no place for you to

be!"

Leaving, the moon said... "O no, you must be

crazy,

fortune waits here, but door you won't open to

see!"

If you are desiring this world, you are a mere

hireling:

if paradise you seek, heart from truth, is a far

thing.

You foolishly find happiness in both worlds:

you'll be forgiven, unaware of Joy, Love can

bring.

For Love, gamble your life... if you are a real man
too:

or, go on your way, we'll have nothing to do with
you.

One whose heart's mean won't gain this state…

you seek God, but on road, getting lost is all you
do.

Although, for awhile, Fate on you, seems to

smile;

don't call Fate friend, she will humble you in

awhile.

Fate suddenly starts to intoxicate you, then

her false breast given to another lover, is her

style.

Down flowing river a boat is carried

fast;

it seems to the mind, the reeds hurry

past...

at moment like this from world we go

and it seems to us, this world doesn't

last.

People say, that Paradise above is waiting

for us…

wine to drink all day and dark eyes, loving,

for us!

We spend days with wine and beauties… for

finally like that, in Paradise they're staying,

for us!

The birds all went to Solomon* with their
cries:
"Why, why don't you ever the nightingale
criticise?"
Nightingale answered: "Do not be upset,
three months I sing, nine in mouth tongue
lies."

The essence is, in poverty… every thing else is
accidental:
heart's ease is poverty, all else… soul's disease:
all!
This world's a complete delusion, winter snow:
the only real treasure is poverty… the spiritual
goal.

You, who like the crow, love winter's cold and
snow,
are exiled from garden's rose and nightingale's
show.
To heart take this moment for it soon will pass:
you search with many lamps, eyes, after it does
go.

Your days of childhood have passed and youth
too…
old age is upon your head, so with this world be
through.
Three days you've been promised as a guest here:
kind sir your time's over… get up, pass on, won't
you?

Every one, of the Almighty's Omnipotence, are

all

playthings:

the All-powerful is rich: us, beggars we beg for

mere

'things'.

Why do we keep wanting more than the other

has?

Don't we stand equally... before palace that is

our

King's?

If it is for gold you're seeking, your life to gold is
sold...

if you're greedy for bread, soul's led by bread: be
told.

Listen to this subtlety, make sure you know it...

whatever you set the heart on, you become that,
manifold.

We do not pay regards to any country, we are a

kalandar: *

we're no lord of palace… without a gate, we're a

beggar.

No, no… we are like a brush that is held by the

Painter…

it is impossible to understand where we stand…

where?

We do not care about satin, or in any purse some

silver:

we are at ease with pain... and unaffected by any

terror.

As long as time's existing we to God's law, bow:

heart does this happily, not grudgingly, as you

are.

Do you think that I do whatever I'm wanting

to…

or, each moment, my hand lets me do what I

do?

I lie like a pen, waiting for Writer to take up,

or, I am like a ball, a prisoner of my mallet…

You!

You are the spring and all of us, we are the

grasses:

You're the King and we're all your beggars,

yes!

You are the Voice... we all merely an echo:

You, seek us... why don't we go, into Your

Oneness?

That heavenly rider went by and in the air, dust

rose...

that One went fast but that dust stays where it,

arose.

Your vision is straight forward... gaze on ahead:

that One's dust is here, but in the Infinite, is in

repose.

When I see that one's face that has seen Your

Grace...

O God, radiance fills my heart and eyes in my

face:

this is a truth... if one, through eternity, gazes

on Your beauty, amazement that one will fully

embrace.

Who was that one who said the immortal soul's

dead,

and how dare that one say, that the sun of hope

fled?

That enemy of the sun who stood up on his roof

covered his eyes and cried out, "Look, the sun is

dead."

Ah no, it is O so late, and upon the sea

we are…

and desperately seeking a shore to see…

we are.

It's night and in the cloudy sky's no star:

but sailing with God's grace… obviously

we are.

Inside your soul another Soul resides,

go look for it:

inside your mountain, a Mine hides,

go look for it!

The *Sufi, that one seeks as he goes...

go look for it:

not outside; from the heart He guides,

go look for it.

Who is that One that raises up the spirit,

Who?

Who in the beginning created life, gave it:

Who?

Who hoods eyes like a falcon for just a bit:

Who?

Soon that One will let me hunt prize… It!

Who?

From Noah* our inheritance is... the Ark of

deliverance,

in it we sail into middle of sea of life's great

expanse.

Out of that sea, in heart a plant is growing...

and like where heart is, it is a pure, limitless

infiniteness.

Look, I'll discover another purpose in my mind,

another:

look, I'll a more beautiful one as beloved find…

another!

God is my witness… love is not nearly enough:

after autumn's blossoming, a spring I will find…

another!

If your soul finds peace… in love, for just one

moment,

where in ranks of lovers do you stand… in the

present?

Prick like thorn so like rose beloved might pin

you to that breast, and in hair braid you, to it

compliment.

If it is… that the road that the lover is travelling

ends at only one place, death, and then nothing…

then that tale is false: for love is a river flowing,

containing immortality for lovers to be drinking.

Fearless speed of falcon... and pride of tiger

take:

in chase be splendid, in battle never the rear

take.

Nightingale's song, peacock's beauty never

take:

it's only melodious voice, all show... there!

Take?

I'm still seeking that Friend, as I hurry my
feet…
life is coming to an end, sleep my eyes still
meet.
If it should happen that the Friend I should
greet,
all the years gone… can I regain, and make
sweet?

God forbid His sword or arrow fill hearts with

fear,

or that we are afraid of chained feet, or head on

spear.

We rush about so much, as we taste hell's fires

near,

frightened whatever others say will bring more

fear.

Heart and spirit are not as fine, as Your form, divine…

sugar not as sweet as Your kiss, when our lips combine.

Sun and moon spend ages as they circle on their line:

turning, they seek in dark, light… Your night's sign.

O heart's delight, You have gone: but, never to

depart

will be Your form from these eyes, or, from this

heart.

I travel through the world hoping You'll finally

come to me and reveal how my way to You can

start.

If, on the right path your way home you cleverly

find,

a light shall shine forth and to heaven you will be

inclined.

Heaven's throne's your place of rest: it's a shame

like some shadow in the dust, your face you have

reclined?

You aren't really water, and you aren't

clay:

unlike water and clay… you are, on the

Way.

A river's the form, its stream is the soul:

You travel forever… and over both hold

sway.

For a time, as I wanted it… I claimed to be
myself:

I heard its name, but I did not see… the true
Self:

involved with self, I didn't see worth of that
Self…

then, I left myself behind and then I had the
Self!

Those with no chattels who experience mystical

ecstasy;

nightly, they secretly live with One they love…

completely.

Get up and leave us now, you ones alien to our

company,

for, any strangers in this blessed night… cause

agony.

Wool-carder Hallaj* who, " I am the Truth,"

declared;

swept God's dust from each road, on which he

stepped.

And when that one in the sea of non-existence

dived,

won for us the pearl when he "I'm the Truth,"

said.

If you have ears to hear this message

clearly...

tie your heart to that One, leave self

immediately.

Be silent when you see that vision...

perfectly,

whatever speech can declare, is there

to see!

This intoxication of ours is not in need of any
wine
nor harp or flute, we all need to feel joy that's
divine.
Without winebringer, beauty, minstrel or reed,
we are like drunkards… ecstatic, exultant and
sublime.

Glory be to You O God, O radiant pearl,

glowing...

we seem to be, You and I... opposites, in

everything!

I am Your good fortune that never sleeps,

and You are mine who never from sleep is

waking.

Night, and what a fire in my chest's raging:

strange!

And now it looks to me like day is dawning:

strange!

In the eye of Love, day and night don't exist:

this eye of Love, this one's eye is blinding...

strange!

That knowledge that your knot can be undoing,

seek:

it, before your soul your body will be leaving…

seek!

Give up the illusion that looks like the Reality:

that Being that is looking like this non-being…

seek!

All of the conspirators of secrets are intoxicated,

tonight…

they are locked away in privacy with Beloved,

tonight.

Stranger to Existence, keep away from this place,

strangers nearby is a stupidity; better left unsaid,

tonight.

That one, not caring for more or less; peaceful

is that one:

one not caring about poverty or wealth; so full

is that one.

Free from the people and sorrows of the world,

having no relationship to himself... none at all,

is that one

Those bitter words of Yours, that so break this

heart...

really, from that mouth is it proper for them to

depart?

Your sweet lips a bitter word... never uttered:

such misfortune, is from my bad luck... just to

start!

That wild, free Love, off into the desert was
dashing...
this heart saw it, and by its glory... it, was
recognising.
Heart: "If I'm ever let go, from restrictions;
due to face of Love, in love, I'll be instantly
falling!"

It is quite true, that love…so full of kindness

is:

human nature's cruelty, a problem, I stress…

is.

You keep telling me that your lust's love: but

a long way from lust to love… my emphasis,

is.

O soul, your Beloved, you've an understanding

Who it is:

and you, O heart, your Guest, you're knowing

Who it is?

O body, you who're desperately seeking a way:

One pulls you in… see Who you keep seeking,

Who… it is!

O Kind Sir, your concerns are with glory and

beauty,

you think of your gardens and fields, harvests,

obviously.

Nothing but the world of Unity consumes us:

we think only of, "There is no god, but God,"

constantly.

O you, Truth seeker, if on this path you have

determination…

if in your mind you've the desire to reach the

destination…

do you know Men of Truth's key, successful

incantation?

This: their joyful, "There's no god but God,"

recitation.

Leave here, reason... there's no one who's wise
here:

if you became a hair, there is nothing your size,
here!

Here, it is daytime and a lamp that in day is lit
isn't even a small flame, when the sun in sky is
here.

All of this wine without any goblets…

who are they for:

we have caught the bird, so these nets…

who are they for?

Each moment to lovers are offered much

sugar and pistachios, almonds in duets…

who are they for?

My chest is on fire is nurtured by my Master's
teaching;
this fever of mine today's because of Master's
doing.
I'll give up all Physician has told me to give up;
but, wine or sugar that from Beloved of lover, is
coming!

Not from that red wine, is this drunkenness

of mine...

in casket of love is found wine's forgetfulness

of mine.

You've arrived here to be pouring wine to me:

but, I'm one having wine... invisible, no less,

of mine.

Every type of misconduct, can be attributed to me…

I'm an infamous lover, passionate, a drunkard, obviously.

My Friend, because You're my goal above all, why complain? Because of You… we all keep existing!

That Friend, continues to shut Union's door,

to this one…

that One loves giving pain to heart, as before,

to this one.

I'll now sit at that One's door broken-hearted:

Friend can't ignore giving help: what's in store

to this one?

Than an impatient lover, a more wretched one is

where?

This love of mine is a difficulty, without answer,

whatsoever.

Remedy for love's agony isn't patience or fakery:

in a love that's real there's no faith, no cruelty...

never!

When result of my suffering, remedy's answer
becomes…
depression… exultation, disbelief… a believer
becomes.
Path's obstructions were body, soul and heart:
body… heart, heart… soul, soul beloved of lover
becomes.

My companion... the soul, now a stranger

is...

my doctor... reason, now, even more crazier

is.

In ruined places monarchs hide their treasure:

because of treasure, our ruin even shabbier...

is.

Unless one denies ones self, one's self will never

die…

that one, won't realise secret that in Unity does

lie.

The secret's not God in form, but being selfless:

all else is boasting, patently another lie one may

try.

Because I am completely satisfied with being a

nothing…

why do you keep advising me to become my own

being?

If on that Last Day 'me' Nothing's sword slays,

if someone weeps for me, with greatest joy I'll be

laughing!

While You and Your heart are far off with me

You are...

far in walking distance and impossible to see,

You are.

You'll never be united with me, until with me

You are...

on Love's path either I'm far off, or obviously

You are.

As you are no slave why not call yourself a
king...

whatever you aim for, why not fly high that
thing?

And when you are set free of yourself... and
everything,

beat the drum of Divinity... for self you are
losing.

If you become the prey of God, grief flies from

you…

if you keep hunting your self, 'you' stay tied…

too.

Understand that your own life's a veil covering

You…

while in your self You dwell, the Work is never

through.

That wine I drank where the spirit is the
cup,
demolished reason... intellect, mad, gave
up!
Aflame a candle came, and set me on fire:
in its flare, sun like moth, in ecstasy does
sup!

The true worth of the mind is to be found in
madness...
Love's madman is beyond all reason, this I
stress!
One who by grief and knowledge finds heart,
thousand times his self will state... less than
less!

That everyone is led by some kind of stupidity

is true...

that all I know, has head full of melancholy...

is true.

Desire's thread that rises from love in the heart

winds truly: that few know where its home be,

is true.

On that day love's disturbance in my heart

is,

spirit upon naked feet fleeing from the start

is.

One's mad who thinks of me reason any part

is...

or wise, who from mad me... quickly to depart

is.

When in this chest Your flame of Love was set
alight...

all but Love in my heart was by Love consumed
outright.

Brain's subtlety, school, or any book I found not
right:

I learnt hard the poet's craft, so verse in rhyme I
write.

Sun, whose light tries vying with Your beauty,

is where:

breeze, trying to catch waft of Your perfumery...

is where?

Brain in body's citadel that seems beyond defeat,

the moment that it enters Your street, its sanity

is where?

When, the love for You took hold in the mind of

heaven,

agony and much noise arose in the great space,

then.

When the whole world soars into the Spiritual,

Your love drawing all to You: up and down are

forgotten!

With the wine the lover must be... night and
day,
'til reason and shame's veil is torn completely
away.
Why keep drinking? Wine, has nothing left in
my mind to take, that reason didn't give up in
dismay!

Love visited me... said: "You should go against

reason,

against spirit... with me alone you should make

habitation.

Time and again I came to you, and I was gone."

Listen, now I am in Love's heart... no more any

destination.

Where is mind of the lover? In the wind's wake,

is where!

Where's clever man's brain? Silver, gold to take,

is where!

Where's the priceless rose? In paradise to forsake

is where!

Where's brushwood stay? In hell's fires to bake...

is where!

There is a desert beyond faith and faithfulness,

there is…

in that space, in this tired heart, more not less

there is.

For one coming here, in the end, a peacefulness

there is:

this is because neither faith nor unfaithfulness,

there… is.

There's a place beyond this world of faith and
infidelity...
in it is no grace, no freshness... and not even
beauty.
One with ambition to in such a peaceful home
be...
must renounce life and the heart in one's chest,
gratefully.

Until college and minaret are both in ruins,

laying…

the kalandar* is not yet free to his trade be

plying.

Until disbelief is faith and infidelity one is

believing,

no one is true until death and to only God

resigning.

As salt dissolves in ocean, in God's sea I was
immersing…
beyond faith and disbelief, doubt and certainty
disappearing.
Suddenly in heart, a star clear and bright was
shining…
all the heavenly suns, in that star's light were
vanishing!

As my essence to that Infinite Sea is
turning...
my atoms, subliminal, in splendour are
shining!
See... that on the road of Love I blaze!
A moment... moment of all my days is
enveloping!

Since that beauty stole heart, from my loving

that One,

by alchemy my dust that One is transmuting:

that One!

With a thousand hands in lands I was seeking

that One...

hands stretched to feel, my heels were holding,

that One.

I promised again and again that as long as I'm

living...

from the straight and narrow path I will not be

straying.

Now, whenever my eyes either right or left I'm

turning...

right or left... where I look, that face I love, I'm

seeing!

If you want essence of the Friend revealed to

you…

go to the centre: of fine skin… have nothing to

do.

Friend's essence is veiled… many folds cover:

Friend in Being is drowned, all beings in there

too.

The sun of Your fair cheek, rises beyond any

sky…

it's impossible to describe Your beauty: why

try?

Your Love, in my soul, found another home:

Love, living far beyond my soul, and stars on

high.

Into my heart Your Love came and departed

happily...

on returning, put its baggage down and fled,

happily.

I cried... "Please, why not stay a few days?"

Your Love sat, and now cannot be removed:

happily!

I am a mountain, the echo of the Beloved is my

cry…

I'm an image: Beloved painted the one that am

I.

It may seem to you… what was just said, said

I?

When key turns in the lock, lock's sound does

certify.

Where river of the Friend races, none is listless

there…

that One's garden of roses, not one thorn, does

bear.

It is said that there is a door from heart to heart:

no need of doors, no walls are between there and

here.

That Friend inside this heart of mine, is

living…

breath of a thousand bodies, my flesh is

inhabiting.

In a wheat grain a thousand bundles are

waiting:

hundred worlds inside a needle's eye are

lying.

A hidden treasure in this world of clay,

we are...

eternally creating, whatever doing today

we are.

Because passing the night of flesh's sway

we are...

life's immortal tide and Guide upon Way

we are.

Ever since I first heard Love's famous story

told…

in its cause with heart, soul and eyes, I was

bold.

I said, "Perhaps Beloved and lover are two:"

but… no, the two were One… but eyes saw

twofold.

Of the great mystery of God... the treasury

we are:

sea where lies the prize, pearl of immortality,

we are.

From end to never an end of Being's eternity,

we are...

yes, sitting on the throne of God's Majesty,

we are.

O heart of mine, when you see that Beloved,
immediately
on seeing, extinguish yourself, do not sigh…
half-heartedly.
It is true… that when sun's face shines forth
gracefully,
if the candle is not dead, it's extinguished…
instantly!

Of the book of God... really a copy

you are:

a mirror showing the King's beauty

you are.

All that God ever created is... united:

all sought, finding in own heart, really

you are.

You are in my sight, or the light be seeing,

could I?

You are in my mind, or insanity be having,

could I.

Wasn't Your Love living there? As I can't

tell where it is… could I, there be staying,

could I?

Master, You'll not see me here with sleepy

eyes...

in a year You'll see me likewise, I don't tell

lies.

Nightly, as I lie for a moment, watch me...

You'll not catch me, even when dawn does

rise.

A few nights until dawn, heart still watching,

don't you sleep...

the moon wakes up, and the sun is now setting:

don't you sleep.

Your pail in the shadows of the well be lowering,

don't you sleep...

it's possible that you will up from it be coming...

don't you sleep!

Last night in love, until the morning's pale
dawning,
heart of mine was my companion... never
sleeping.
To You, with the dawn... came its bright
shining:
quickly... eyes bloody, cheeks with tears
encrusting.

Please tell me, the night has disappeared,

where?

has it gone back to where it first appeared,

there?

When, O night, you return to your home...

take some news with grace, of how I fared,

here!

Every night flowers are blossoming in the
sky...
in the peaceful Infinite, fully at peace am
I.
From my heart sighs rise by the hundred...
my heart cold and dark is on fire with each
sigh.

My Sweetheart came to me last night, quite

suddenly…

that One with such sweet lips, spoke to me,

provocatively…

that One shook me where I lay and cried out:

"Stop sleeping! You haven't seen *this* sun…

obviously!'

Love has never rested and has never been

sleeping…

Love, at those who sleep deeply, is never

looking.

I'll not relate any more… for it is a word

Love has never said, and that, none… is

hearing.

If, during one night you do not sleep until

daylight…

on your bright spirit the moon will throw,

moonlight.

Fountain of Life is in the dark: don't sleep,

right?

Perhaps with this, one night you'll taste…

delight.

If you came to fight, with the Ethiopian of this
night,
open in your chest that night that is there, O so
tight!
When you've come to move around Love's altar,
be witness that Love's altar moves... with you in
sight!

Tonight, the moon of Love is full... full of bright

wonder:

the One who delights me, looks from roof at this

lover.

Tonight, heart, remember your Creator, yourself

lower...

tonight, like cup, all sleep you are forbidden, O

drinker.

Do you know what is night… listen, I'll tell you

honestly:

night keeps lovers apart from heart's strangers…

nightly.

This particular night when moon's home with

me,

I'm drunk… moonlight's my lover and the night's

… crazy!

Borne by Love's breath, our boat sailed out from
death…

when Love's wine unites hearts, night's bright by
stealth!

Why is it, that wine that by my faith has blessed
wealth,

will always slake this thirst of mine, 'til dawn's
death?

This drunkenness of mine is not from a crimson

wine...

my wine's not found in a wine, but in a passion,

divine!

Ah my friend, was it your intention to spill this

wine?

Wine that makes me laugh, was never of earth's

design.

Winebringer, I asked, "Pour us that clear, sweet

wine:

in Your cup for outsiders, there is wine that's...

divine."

The Friend replied, "In circling skies is a wind!"

Until that wind comes up, until the end... pour

wine!

The dawn has yet to rise, hey, the morning cup
bring...

bright lamp of the wine, moon and sun... will be
outshining!

Bring me that liquid fire O Winebringer, and be
setting

fire to this darkness and let all, eventually, it be
consuming.

See, from Friend of heart desire's we come, wine
carrying...
and this flame of divine Love, the soul on fire is
lighting.
Until this world ends no dreamer such nights is
dreaming
as these nights, 'til the dawn's first light we are
spending.

As beat of *tabor,* the large drum, in air begins to

rise...

my unfortunate heart like some prisoner... escape

tries.

And then from that beating drum, a hidden voice

cries...

"You poor, tired soul... come, the road this way

lies."

Listen as the lute's playing and know what it is saying…

"Here, here, come with me… road to you I'll be showing.

I'm wrong, you have to… to at last at home be coming…

look, look, you must go until the answer you're finding."

When the soul is hurting, and yet it can still

listen…

a song from the heart shall all of its suffering

lessen.

See the wonderful rose in my heart blooming,

it has no colour but its perfume it now reveals

again.

When the minstrels are singing this heart's

fluttering…

like lightning darting through the clouds at

spring.

Drums are silent and the singers are here…

singing:

come, sweet Venus… merciful God, lute be

playing.

Listen to the minstrel, singing about Love's

mystery:

while flute's reed weeps... tell all the hearts

story.

O listen carefully to minstrel's quiet advice:

he

whispers... "Don't go unless the veil covers

completely."

That bowl to me, that a broken soul will mend,

bring…

cup that king and slave into ecstasy will send,

bring.

Tune mode so heart's food will eternally blend:

bring…

because a trumpet of death will a new life send,

bring!

The Angel of Death speaks, and my heart is

happy…

I rise from the valley of death, cry to the skies,

happy!

None has an idea what happened to me then:

how that invisible messenger made soul arise,

happy!

As long as I am alive, I am the slave of Your
hair…

Your wild, flowing curls this sick mind, make
better.

O reed, weep: your sad song intoxicates soul.

O lute, don't soften tune, today I eat… what I
hear!

How long like drum, under Your tyranny will I

groan...

like *rebeck's* sigh, how long for Your infidelity

moan?

You say: "I'll caress you like a lute, on breast,

alone,"

but, I'm not a flute on which You've already

blown.

When that One plays music I have to clap my
hands:
I was created crazy… I laugh at what dignity
demands.
I proved that One's heart, made my heart do
handstands,
and created me into whatever form that One
commands.

Than Time...more bloodthirsty and killing:

Your eyes...

sharper than spears are lashes, surrounding

Your eyes.

Tell me again secret that You'd whispered...

it's harder for ears to hear when I am seeing

Your eyes.

The sun of Your face, than the one in the sky,

is beyond…

like Your beauty which to tell, or to even try,

is beyond.

Inside this soul of mine Your Love is living…

it's strange it, world, soul that in me does lie,

is beyond.

Our sun and stars and our moon that is full

is that One...

our garden, home, chair and plot plentiful...

is that One.

Where we pray, patience, fasts sure or fitful,

is that One...

festival, Ramadan, *Koran night, bountiful,

is that One.

In this search, the sane and the crazy

are the same...

on Love's path, strangers and family,

are the same.

To one given wine of Beloved's union,

the *Kaaba* * and idol-temple obviously

are the same.

Any trick that I ever tried in this loving You

was useless...

any heart's blood I drank alone toasting You

was useless.

There's no remedy I can discover for this pain:

Who'd cure me? This pain from needing You,

was useless!

In Love... where only eternity's wine, one is
drinking,
nothing leads to Eternal Life... but, life to be
surrendering.
I said, "I want to know You... then, I'll die:"
You replied, "That one knowing me, is never
dying!"

There is, in the gathering of lovers, one special

regulation…

that love's wine gives a special hangover later

on.

That knowledge one might gather in any school

is one thing: love's something quite different, a

revelation.

My heart, beats in my breast, only from grieving
for You…
it's a stranger to others, close friend of suffering
for You.
My suffering for You is a benefit to my heart, or
how can my lonely heart grief be accommodating,
for You?

Heart went to be with One who's happy without

me…

grief's unpleasant: for that One, near me is being

unhappy.

That One requests my life… a few days I wait:

life is not valuable, but that request is worth a

treasury.

That kingly One, my mediator for all my sinning

has gone…

the night, better than a thousand moon's shining

has gone.

If that One comes back and sees I've gone, say…

"Like You, that one who off to road was going

has gone!"

Sword of eternity is carried by hands of Men
of God...
the ball of eternity lies in the polo-stick's bend
of God.
From that form that is alight like Mount Sinai*
seek to light your way, that One's the dividend
of God.

Your Love is so skilful and so wise…

why is this?

Your kindness is so subtle I surmise,

why is this?

If love is bad, to burn in it my joy lies,

why is this?

If love's good, all these cries and sighs:

why is this?

Reason suddenly came, and tried to advise

the lovers...

sat on the path, tried to away from it prise

the lovers.

It found no room in their heads for advice...

it left, after kissing feet of 'no compromise':

the lovers.

If this whole world was full of

grieving...

one clutching love wouldn't be

suffering.

Witness... an atom patient in

loving

became a universe and all it is

containing!

If someone is ashamed of this person and that

person,

one has to try to cover up the mistakes of each

one.

But, if one has to reveal the bad and the good

one has to show a face of iron, like a mirror, to

everyone.

Even a one who is not crazy through desire

doesn't exist…

one without such an idea in the mind's eye

doesn't exist.

This ardour giving rise to this strong desire

is obvious but invisible, so it's said this fire

doesn't exist.

As well as this language, another
have I...
as well as heaven and hell... other
have I.
Us free-spirited have special souls:
real gem, from a mine that's better,
have I.

That Beauty that is neither above nor below

is where?

That Soul that's neither here or not on show

is where?

No, "Here, there!" That One, high and low

is where?

That One's the world... one who does know,

is where?

A drunkard opened the door and us was

joining...

that crystal cup from hand to hand was

passing:

it suddenly fell down, into pieces it was

smashing...

it's possible with many drunkards, to be

lasting?

My heart is weaker, from its suffering for You,

every day...

Your pitiless heart seems to hate me more, too,

every day.

You left me alone, my suffering for You didn't:

it's true this suffering has more faith than You,

every day.

The perfume of You, out from my nose,

never went:

The image of Your face from my eyes...

never went.

Life passed, wanting You night and day;

my life did end, but for You my desires...

never went!

That mote, that only with the sun did

dance...

took the cash and did not give hope a

chance.

What mind that was full of Your Love

did not like the top of the willow-tree,

dance?

That one sleeps who is not aware of that

One...

to one aware of that One, sleep does not

come.

Each night Love's whispering in my ears:

"Misery comes to one asleep without that

One!"

That One who this one into the world's fire
placed...
hundreds of flames on my tongue's bonfire,
placed.
When on all sides the flames surrounded me
I sighed... then a hand on my mouth my Sire
placed.

That one who knew You, has for life...

what need:

for any children, a house, or any wife...

what need?

You drive one crazy, give both worlds:

Your mad one for both worlds strife...

what need?

That Friend, who the doctor's heart is
stealing,
can this doctor for that One, a cure be
prescribing?
If that One shows an atom of beauty,
O God, this doctor will need a doctor
arriving!

From the fire of Your Love, being young again

flares up…

so much Beauty in one's breast there and then,

flares up!

Do it, if You wish to kill me: it is lawful, do it!

From those killed by Beloved, real Life again…

flares up!

In this Love of Yours the sea with desire is
boiling...
and all of the clouds at Your feet pearls are
strewing.
In Your Love, a lighting bolt has hit earth:
smoke in the sky is from that bolt You are
throwing!

My dear, in love, never ever a loser
you will be!
Can you be dead when life's creator
you will be?
Originally, you came here from sky:
eventually, ascending much further
you will be.

Except for a flag, of my patience's army,

nothing stayed:

except for grief, of everything left of me,

nothing stayed.

Most unbelievable is I'm still breathing:

from love, except for a breath... certainly

nothing stayed.

Because Your face thieved a whole world's

heart...

what's the use of staying at home, why not

depart?

Didn't You know when You became a moon

You'd be seen through the world? Not that

smart!

Today, our Beloved desires us to be…

in a frenzy:

that One wants more, more than we…

in a frenzy!

If not true… why be tearing our veils?

That One wants us… openly, to all be

in a frenzy!

This is not the night to out of our house be

going...

to be leaving Beloved, and to strangers be

meeting.

This is a night when all of our dear friends

have to drunkenly, into the fire of love, be

walking.

O heart, the sign of morning in the evening,

who has seen…

a true lover with good reputation following,

who has seen?

You scream out that you've been burned…

do not do it! A raw one who's still burning,

who has seen?

O graceful cypress, may autumn winds not blow

to You…

vision of the world, may the evil eye none show

to You.

You who are the Soul of the hearth and heaven:

may only much peace and many blessings, flow

to You.

One who gets mixed up in Your Love for even a

moment

will experience personal disaster to an incredible

extent.

When *Mansur Hallaj revealed the Secret of

Love...

he was hung by the throat of rope of that zealous

establishment.

Pleasure and happiness aren't flourishing

without love…

grace, beauty are not a part human living,

without love.

Many drops in a sea from clouds may fall

but no drop a pearl will ever be becoming,

without love.

Unless any one's self, completely non-existent

becomes...

any one a knower of God's Unity, to no extent

becomes.

God's Unity isn't after death but self's death:

from false claims no lie a truth that is relevant

becomes.

Your generosity, does what even the sea

doesn't do...

Your kindness, putting off 'til 'eventually'

doesn't do.

To ask You for anything is not necessary:

one, ask for light from the sun, obviously

doesn't do.

After eyesight's gone, one's angry speech

has any worth:

after heart's bleed dry, one's faith's reach

has any worth?

When grief one has consumes one's body,

that reviving speech that one could teach,

has any worth?

Filling this head of mine is a wonderful
longing…
my heart is a bird, that into the blue is
soaring.
Every atom in me, is moving by itself:
perhaps that Beloved… everywhere is
walking.

Lovers can lose both of the worlds in only a
moment...
a hundred years of life they can lose... in an
instant.
For a breath they'll pass a hundred states...
for one heart, a thousand lives they'll have
spent.

Those on the Path who know the secret of
meaning,
from eyes of all who are short-sighted are
hiding.
Also, that one knowing the truth became
a believer, but was by people called... non-
believing.

I feel humble before those who themselves are

knowing...

who, every moment, hearts from the false are

freeing;

themselves from any attribute and essence are

emptying,

and "I'm the Truth" on board of their being are

reading.

My heart boils over, while trying to reach Your

exuberance…

to reach Your consciousness I lost of my self all

sense.

It's drinking poison so as to reach Your honey…

it's a ring, so it can reach Your ear, to be held in

suspense.

Stay awake, for God's Grace is coming...

suddenly,

to a heart that's wide awake it is arriving,

suddenly!

Make your being's tent empty of yourself:

and when it is empty, the King is entering,

suddenly!

Some time among the population I was

spending…

a sign of faithfulness in them, I was not

discovering.

It's better from population's eyes I hide,

like water in iron and fire in the stone is

hiding.

A perfect Love and with me that Sweetheart
is,

my heart full of words... but tongue split apart
is!

Has there ever been a more unique situation...

I'm O so thirsty, while before me a water-cart
is?

To take my Self out from myself,

is my desire:

to liberate my self with my Self,

is my desire.

I'm chained to the Path's stops:

release from chains of false self,

is my desire!

It is a party… do not be here without

tambourine…

get up, the drum beat, we are Mansur*

obviously.

We're intoxicated, but not from wine:

we're far from anything you thought to

be!

As long as I've desired, all I wanted was
You…
the table of love I decorated as Love… as
You!
Last night I had a dream, but it I forgot…
now all I know is I was drunk, but not as
You!

When that One played music my hands I loudly

clapped:

my lack of reason made me do it... I at dignity

laughed!

That One's heart, now I know this... my heart

stirred:

that One created me... when in me that music

moved.

You are my shining sun and a mere mote am

I:

You are the only cure I have... of grief I may

die.

I'm flying to You, though I have no wings...

I'm merely a mote of straw, into Your light I

fly.

The light of heaven is this dusty, old body

of mine...

angels are jealous when this flight they see

of mine.

The cherubs are all so envious of this purity

of mine...

and devils are on the run, from this bravery

of mine.

When I go... circling around

You,

crown's on cup... wine flows

too.

I'm amazed at Your kindness

to

me... and blinded like Moses*

too!

Inside this place today one can see
dancing...
such a divine grace of perfection of
moving.
And if of such dancing you may be
disapproving...
moon... a ray, in your dull heart is
shining.

Tonight, I wander around the abode of the
Friend...
until dawn in the Friend's home my time I
spend.
It was decreed by my Friend to be so, that
my head be a cup and from it... drinks my
Friend.

Tonight, every heart seeking the moon's pale
light...
like fair Venus, everywhere is causing much
delight.
I almost die from despair to press those lips:
silence! God knows what is passing on this
night!

Leap up, leap up, for the soul's rhyme is near

by...

drum's sweet beat is in time with the reed's

sigh!

The old fires of grief leap up, even higher...

tell your sorrow, "Now it's time for tears to

transpire."

Get up now... move around the Master of our

salvation:

like wind blowing pilgrims about Mecca's holy

destination.

Why are you bound up in sleep like earth's clay?

Through moving you'll discover each blessing's

revelation.

While the sun of the spirit is so brightly

shining…

like a mote the adept with delight keeps

dancing!

I hear some people say, "It is some devil

whispering:"

some devil that gently, the spirit's life is

taking.

That drunken one who saw me clapped hands,

shouted…

"Look… our pilgrim is back, penance has been

resisted!"

Yes, but the penitent was like a glass-maker

who spent much time working then found it

smashed!

That one's no lover who isn't like the soul,
agile...
or like star at night, around moon doesn't
circle.
Now listen to me, because lying isn't my
style...
unless breeze blows flag can't dance, even
awhile.

I shouted out, "The mystical dance begins...

get up!"

You... "Be off, your servant's heart sickens,

get up!"

I replied, "Even if dead, you will live again...

our Jesus* by God's miracle, new life begins,

get up!"

Every single atom dancing on field or in the
air...
look closely at it, like crazy us, it's spinning
there.
Every single atom, whether happy or not...
keeps circling the Sun, in ecstasy... beyond
compare.

That One in whom my soul lives circles my

heart...

around my heart and blissful soul goes my

Sweetheart.

In my earthly bed I raise head like a tree...

for the Fountain of Life, washes my every

part.

O day, come out... the motes are happily

dancing:

through night the spirits are delightfully,

dancing.

Come close, I'll whisper that One's name:

that One, from whose light, all spheres be

dancing!

That Beloved, like the sun, keeps on
shining...
like mote around sun the lover keeps
hovering.
When breath of Love that on high is
quivering...
forest is entranced, young boughs are
dancing.

I thieved this way of spinning, from my

spirit...

I found it in my form, into soul I moved

it.

They say, "It is better to rest, be calm:"

they can have their calm and rest: every

bit.

If these two hands above my head I am

clapping,

the wine's flowing in my veins: don't be

disapproving.

These agile feet from fortune's wheel are

leaping...

yes, from good and from evil I have been

escaping.

I'm drunk with Your love, not from opium or

wine…

I'm mad, in one crazy one looks for manners

fine?

From inside my soul, a hundred torrents do

combine…

heavens in surprise, stop, to see me spin in

line.

Get up… and travel to where one finds the

Beloved:

feet to that One a with fine face and name

tread.

Leap out from this trap that's stopping you

and if sent away from door, come in by roof

instead.

When You come to me at midnight, feet

stamping…

until the dawn Your brow with delight is

glowing.

By hand, curl by curl, night's hair You are

freeing…

in this land You are without peer… I am

declaring.

Last night you were drunk, my heart, and left

quickly…

what wine was it, that today you worse off

be?

Were you joyfully dancing like a green leafy

tree…

or, like the dawn did you wait upon the sun

faithfully?

I was an atom and You made me tall as a

mountain…

I lagged behind, now I am the leader of all

men.

My heart was sick and You made me well

again…

to be a *rend*, dance for Your love there and

then.

Those on your trail... following you, night and

day:

those hunters quick to hit, who wish to, you...

slay;

to cut you from your Love, is their will... their

way,

if you will not move they will draw you along

anyway.

Robbers wait on the road, so don't go out

alone...

there are many enemies, but a soul's only

one.

The beauty you see you call life and faith:

but to you, some are fair, who are really a

crone.

Beware, beware, for demons are running

everywhere:

with bait and net... your foolish heart to

snare.

Body's happy, holding heart by hem with

care...

it sees the disembodied and of them does

beware.

Causing such bliss in our circle to all...

what is this...

when gone hearts into destruction fall:

what is this?

It comes invisibly, disappears: tell all...

what, is this?

This ecstasy isn't of drum or reed's call.

What is this?

This is not some spring, this some other season

is:

behind each drunken, sleepy, eye another union

is.

Although dance of all boughs in woods going on

is,

each bough dancing from root it's growing upon,

is.

Even if the heavens were heavy with grief and

worry,

the lovers strong and pure grief won't need to

carry.

Mote tapping feet, that on Love's street does

tarry...

has become so mighty the world as his he does

see.

My drunken Beloved came through the door

suddenly,

drank ruby crowned cup, sat, asked for more,

suddenly.

I saw that loose hair: that noose I reached for

suddenly…

face was all eye to look, eye all hand to adore,

suddenly!

When the sprinkling jewels fall out of the
sky…
every atom back to its original source will
fly.
But, by breezes of opposite forces blown,
the atoms run at speed… from the sun on
high.

The first moment the soul wore the body's

clothing...

the full ocean, over with divine grace was

spilling.

When heart's reed the lip's wine was first

tasting,

it played a divine chant as it was ecstasy

experiencing.

The flames of your desires were in my soul,

burning:

waters of your sweetness in my heart were

flowing.

The waters were a mirage and flames, snow

falling…

perhaps back then I was dreaming: now I'm

waking.

This is not the night to be leaving one's true
abode...

for strangers to leave Friend and take to the
road.

Tonight, let true companions take up Love's
load...

in rapture, into Love's flames fall, the self to
explode.

Where You stood on earth joy was new,

there...

You, such joy created that flowers grew

there.

As stars and sphere sung songs for You,

there

moon's eye saw the Star,* You... it knew,

there.

When from the heavens clouds flash God's
lightning…
it is worthless, unless a burning heart it is
striking.
All this whole world needs, is one heart…
bleeding:
so God's bright lightning leaps and sets it
burning!

While I stood outside my beautiful Beloved's
door...
Beloved came and smiled, then smiled some
more.
Beloved pulled me close against that breast,
"Ah, it's my true one, my wise and reverent
lover!"

The dawn's on fire now with the light that
returns…
and one who kept watch, to the way home
turns,
the watchman has his eyes closed in sleep,
but a fiery heart's awake… in heart desire
burns!

The morning breeze is scattering musk as it

blows...

this fragrance from beautiful Beloved's lane

flows.

Don't sleep, get up: don't waste this world!

The caravan soon leaves... sweet scent soon

goes.

Lovers at play gamble both of the worlds
away...
destroy a hundred years, to win joy for a
day:
thousand states for moment's joy they'll
play...
a thousand souls give up to in one Heart
stay.

When Mystery's wind blows, heart's sea is
swirling…
not all hearts are worthy to the Mystery be
knowing.
A heart that Heart's infinite ocean is never
leaving,
this ocean fed by spiritual wine, ecstasy is
experiencing.

When the magic of the form of Adam was
created…
pure spiritual essence inside its clay, was
situated.
When the heavens tore that body's magic,
clay went back to earth, pure to purity was
delegated.

In my snare this strange game lies...

what to do:

my mind spins with rapture... it flies:

what to do?

Heart is free... but, if on road I see a

beauty and to kiss me that one tries,

what to do?

I'm overwhelmed in a sea of imagination,
whirling…

torrent drags me under and in the sea I'm
drowning.

Eyes half-asleep, let that One my spirit be
keeping…

that One of sleepy eye knows in sleep I'm
lying.

Upon each other's face all life long, gazing
were we...
this was how it was, until today... looking
were we.
Until, secret of our hearts, in fear of spies,
with brows speaking... with eyes hearing,
were we.

To heart I whispered, "If you've a chance to be speaking

to Friend... tell of grief that this heart keeps on breaking."

My heart replied, "No... if Friend a chance is giving,

why would I speak... if upon Friend's face I'm gazing?"

What happened last night between us was such

that the tongue cannot tell and for pen is too much!

But when I travel from this old resting-place

telling all will be the winding-sheet's folds I clutch!

This bough, sweetly clustered, some day will
fruit:
the fast-flying falcon will catch prey... by its
pursuit.
That One's beautiful form comes, goes away:
when will it come... in this heart of mine take
root?

If you can have a moment of ecstasy with the
Friend…
yours is a blissful life, if that moment you can
spend.
Careful not to waste such a moment as this...
bliss is rare in a life of pain, on it again do not
depend.

When, upon this plain of death, my foot I

place…

my cry will echo, throughout the whole of

space.

In that nothingness, amazement will take

place…

such a mad mood, the world never heard a

trace.

If I am truly judged, as to my perfection's

worth,

my garment would never leave a mark, on

earth.

I'd quickly fly, tireless, into the heavens…

I'd lift head where the seventh plane gives

birth.

The pathway of God's Messenger,

is Love:

us sons she bore, yes, our Mother...

is Love.

Mother, veiled in us... chaste, pure,

is Love:

hidden from faithless hearts forever,

is Love.

If your life's gone, God offers a new life to

you...

from this life of death, a life eternal that is

new!

In Love is found Fountain of Eternal Life:

so come, in this infinite sea of Love drown

too!

I ask this… if I should die then carry

me

to where my love lies… let me there,

be.

If one kiss on my cold lips I'm given,

don't be amazed if I'm alive again…

instantly!

Life's undying Fountain… is a sprinkle of Your

grace:

moon lighting skies… a pale reflection of Your

face.

I said, "Night's dark: bright the moon I seek."

Your head is night's hair… moon Your cheek's

grace.

O soul, do you have an idea who loves you so
dear,
O heart, do you know who is inside you... so
near?
You who are merely clay seek to find the way:
One draws you near, One who loves you: you
hear?

One will not need a friend who does Friend's

desire…

one knowing profit, won't be bankrupt in the

end.

Moon is bright, so from the night don't flee:

rose has a rare perfume… so thorn one must

defend.

While Your image, envied by the fair, is in my

heart…

in the world is there one who in such joy takes

part?

God, I swear I know one way to live… in bliss!

It's said that many grieve… but, from that, I'm

apart.

When hugging You, Your beauty is my rose...
laughing:

Your form when far from You is heart's faith...
waiting.

For Your sake, my heart and I are constantly
fighting...

both of us states, "I alone that One's love is
owning!"

I said, "Like a pigeon, from Your hand I'll fly
away!"

You replied, "Any such a flight I'll speed up,
anyway!"

I said, "I'll lie at Your feet, lowly... there I'll
stay!"

You replied, "O what glory will be yours that
way!"

Though grief through separating breaks hope's

back...

and beauties shrug at such broken hope, or the

lack

of the same, an ardent lover will never despair:

each will receive the result of each one's aching

back.

One quenching soul's thirst, from Your loving-

cup,

shall take a new life beyond measure, until full

up!

Death stalked me but sensed Your smell near:

fate came to kill me, but in despair gave up its

setup!

A thousand lives are worth less than

loneliness...

freedom's worth more than a world to

suppress.

In your room alone with God as your

witness

is of greater worth than all the earth's

sweetness.

Such Divine Love only goes in search of the

brave...

this Love's a deer that fearlessly a lion does

crave.

Love's temple's Beauty: one that does lovers

enslave...

do you think without you it falls into a ruined

grave?

In Love's Soul, where Your beautiful form

stays…

how can it not stay or move, when there it

lays?

O waning moon, though You're a crescent,

the Perfect Ones shall soon see Your glory

days!

No voice other than Love's in my ear do I
hear...
soul is plundered of sense by joy, loud and
sincere.
Love's invisible pen mixes all the colours,
but the soul still remembers its state... so
clear!

When the eye the rose and anemone is

seeing...

the spinning spheres with its tears it is

filling.

Wines in the jars, for a thousand years

standing...

madness like a year-old love, are never

causing.

When in my hand Your hair I'm holding I'm in
hell...
yet, a strange fear I feel for all that in heaven
dwell.
I am enticed by heaven to take soul from You,
but paradise is far too cramped for my heart's
citadel.

When my fair One first inspired love in my

heart…

I cried such bitter tears, none to sleep could

start.

Now my tears are less and my love is more,

like when the flames rise and the smoke will

depart.

I prayed my beautiful One lives for a hundred

years...

that in my heart I'd feel an arrow of Beloved's

tears.

In dust of Beloved's door my happy heart died:

heart that prayed, "Let Beloved live happily for

years."

Can a lover do anything but humble one's self
make...
at night at Your abode, one's self upon watch
take?
And if he kisses Your chain-like hair don't him
forsake...
doesn't one mad, when mad, such chains try to
break?

The peace of a whole world from love for You ceases...

all life that is will die when to You there is no access.

One smile from You and my heart is gone... I stress...

but I'd not give a thousand lives to live again I confess!

Do not go concealing that You have a great

treasure...

or Your servant will smile, for he knows for

sure.

A blissful bower like Yours is never a prison:

even though upon its gate 'prison' You might

prefer.

Any heart that does not run to One who is
beautiful...
doesn't progress, except towards death, at
all.
That dove that is the prey of Love is happy,
joyful!
No matter how you try to scare is off, it is
resourceful!

Heart came, cried, "This heaviness... is
so long:"

night came... sighed, "That One's hair's
so long!"

The cypress came and wept: "So tallish,
so long!"

That is my life, that One to live, I wish,
so long.

I saw that one only yesterday, with friends,

playing...

so I couldn't that one against my breast be

holding.

So... in that crowded place that face I was

brushing

against, when near... as if in that ear to be

speaking.

I'm like the grape that is trampled
upon...
quickly I fly where Love draws me
on.
You say, "Why circle around me?"
I reply, "No, around Me I circle...
anon!"

Don't think from Love's grief heart any relief

has...

or when far from You I am content with what

is.

From Love's infinite cup my drinking so deep

was...

until all time passes Love's fire in heart raging

is.

I was really happy to die for the love of

You…

and to lay both the worlds at Your feet

too!

Let sun's rays keep shining on our days

to

come… and as clouds roll, let me die for

You.

Flame of my soul, saw I was sick, down-

hearted...

laughing, that One came and sat by my

bed.

That One stroked my brow, head, then

said...

"Poor dear, heart can't stand to see you

sad!"

Last night from kindness, me my loving Friend
visited…

to the night I cried, "This secret can't about be
scattered!"

The night answered with, "Look behind and up
ahead…

when do I bring the light as the sun has already
appeared?"

I'll lay down my head in the dust at Your
doorway...
in twist of Your hair, my heart there I will
lay.
I'm close to death, give Your mouth to sip
away...
so I may sigh away my life on Your lip, to
stay!

I was happy to lie… in the heart of the

pearl:

life's hurricane blew, I ran from wave's

swirl!

The sea's secret I shouted like thunder:

I slept like a spent cloud, curled into a

curl.

You accepted me and yet Your rejection…

I fear;

as I stand near, jealousy's eye's infection,

I fear.

Finally Your love setting on my horizon…

I fear:

I fear the shadow I am casting, on and on

I fear.

If I have not passed the gate of Your palace
before…

it's because I'm afraid of envious ones even
more.

You stay in me, like thoughts in my mind I
store…

to find You, inside my heart I look… for my
Emperor.

I shut my lips and silently said to You many

subtleties...

into ear of Your loving heart I imparted many

secrecies.

In my mind I remember all I said in Your ear:

but what I said, tomorrow I'll show, and You

please.

The dream of the East is Love, the most potent

elixir...

the cloud where ten-thousand lightning strikes

gather.

In my soul Love's glory is like an ocean or even

larger...

and in that ocean all the world's being drowned

forever.

O Lord, when Your fingers strum my heart's

instrument...

hear the deep wailing there and the answer I

invent.

In each ruin that there is, is a treasure that's

different...

Love is the precious prize that in my heart is

evident.

All of you, who due to the world's breath are

alive…

O shame on all of you, to as in a living death

survive.

So, never give up Love, or you will really die:

in Love… be dying, and you will be eternally

alive.

"Be finished with the world, you, running

everywhere...

you're only Mine," this, God to you does

declare.

"Feel for Me, in the end this One who is

fair

will visit you, in your night of solitude...

anywhere."

Love declares, "That one, who life does
sacrifice,
a thousand souls is gaining at a small
price."
Listen to what Love offers by way of its
advice…
Love takes by ear then leads prisoner to
paradise.

Though I try in each way Beloved's whim to

satisfy,

each word Beloved answers is a sword in my

eye.

See how my blood drips from those fingertips:

why does Beloved enjoy washing in my blood,

why?

I asked You this, "What will I do?" "Die!"
You replied.

I said... "Oil in lamp has gone!" "Expire!"
You replied.

I sighed this, "I'm a moth around Your fire
that's flaming high!" "Moth, jump in fire!"
You replied.

My Turk, whose smile my heart finds
beguiling,

whose dishevelled hair soul finds dis-
tressing,

a written note of freedom from me is
taking,

but... I have to be the slave, if it I am
retrieving.

It never occurred to my heart, You'd let me

go:

I dropped load in the mud... You'd laid me

low.

To friends and enemies I boasted about You

so

much... but, I'm ashamed if You now let me

go!

I was modest, chaste too: You made me sing…

eager to be tasting wine and the best at partying.

I used to be sober, dignified, on my mat, praying:

You made me a joke, children mock me… laughing.

If You want to, You can leap... like a

deer:

if You want to, You can strike like a

spear!

While we swing on to this rose-twig

here

like a nightingale, Your heart has no

fear!

You offer Your lip to all the others for

free,

but request payment when it comes to

me.

The sins others do, You are pardoning

completely...

but if I sin, You tie my hands and feet,

tightly.

I'm at war with the day, quickly passing

away:

like river it flows or like wind it's blowing

away.

I'll sit alone tonight as moon is eclipsed...

'til day returns on cup and tray I'm beating

away.

Is anyone more disturbed than an unhappy

lover?

Love is a sickness from which one may not

recover.

Hypocrisy cannot cure it and perseverance

neither...

true love hasn't to do with tyranny or faith

either.

O heart, was dawn's light ever seen in the

evening...

has a real lover ever been safe from others

scorning?

This heart is on fire... I've heard it deeply

sighing:

flames rage to die, for hearts from love are

dying.

Masnavi and *ghazal's* song, the stream

swept away...

that which wasn't my creation, has been

swept away.

Actions... good and bad, my self-denying,

all brought moon's ray: them, moonbeam

swept away.

I will relate to You the story of my

sorrow...

if You cover ears, I will whisper it

somehow.

When grief's mine You're happy I

know...

so, I'll tell You the full tale of my

sorrow!

I said to the doctor, "Cure me, I'm begging
you!"

A knowing look I took, my pulse was taken
too.

That doctor said, "Show me where it pains
you!"

I took that one's hand, my heart I touched it
to.

In a dream I saw a beautiful bringer of
wine...

in that one's hands, I noticed a goblet
shine.

I said, "As you're our Master's slave,

in lieu of that One, take this heart of
mine."

I will never despair, even if You do leave

me

and choose another... although I faithful

be.

I'll grieve for Your love as long as I live:

but in this despair... hope is calling me,

constantly.

Your fair face, makes the world's beauties kowtow…

Your bright brow makes saints before You bow.

I give away all the qualities that I ever had, now…

so I may swim naked in Your stream of joy somehow.

When Your beautiful form comes into my

heart…

my heart that was lost, upon its way does

start.

If when life's passed and a breath's left to

impart,

if Your image comes again, life again will

start.

I call that One wine and cup so bright,

again..

I call that One the gold and silver light

again.

I call that One the snare, game and bait

again…

all I call that One, so name I don't relate

again.

If one should see Your beauty, O One so
kind…
instantly all else will be thrown from the
mind.
What is moon's glare, or Saturn's gleam,
when at noon the Sun shines on angels of
mankind.

In Your perfect light I'm learning to be a
lover:
to Your bright beauty… rhyme and line I
offer.
Though veiled, Your form in my heart's a
dancer…
I look: of lover's and poet's art I become a
learner.

Your beauty's heart's shrine, divine food of spirit…

my soul burnt by sorrow like a candle does spit.

Lift Your veil so I can see Your glory, well-lit…

then I shall, the garment of my heart… tear it!

O moon, whose bright radiance is my life, my

light...

whose divine ray is shining upon my window

tonight!

O heart's beautiful garden, You're my vision

bright...

when will I see You, Your arms holding me

tight?

This heaven and skies…. as far as eyes can
see,

controlled by God's hands are lighter than a
bee.

Each raindrop, or grain… even if it gigantic
be,

are when taken as one are a mere fish in His
sea.

Where I lay my head that One alone is
worshipped,

I humbly kneel before face of He who is
perfected.

Nightingale, lovely garden, idol… song
enraptured,

are all symbols: so seek Him alone to be
adored.

Your infinite Grace, made world of time and

space...

never gave one thought to its intricacies, did

Grace.

One drop came from that flood and into our

place...

in this plain that granary sowed one grain, a

trace.

Although at God's table sits each hungry

grain...

if they eat until eternity, God's table will

remain.

This feast lasting forever... continuing to

sustain

endless feasters clamour, never eaten does

remain.

Your hospitality doesn't boast of two, three
days…
Your tablecloth extends to the earth's ends,
always.
Is not it forgivable, to fall under Your spell?
Around the glow from the candle, the moth
plays.

I'll tell to You clearly a tale no tongue can

tell…

from every ear I will conceal this story so

well.

Although I'll speak where all is heard, I

shall

not let any ear hear but Yours, this tale I

tell.

Now that Your beauty a universe's soul

seizes...

what profit is there sitting at home, *that*

pleases?

When Your beauty first shone on us, an

ecstatic world raised hands to You, in its

happiness.

In the sea I sought a soul and discovered

coral;

underneath the foam, an ocean... I saw it

all:

I went into heart's night... along a narrow

wall,

then I saw light... day of infinite light, as I

recall.

My soul turned face inwards to that
place
where peace reigns: questions...not a
trace!
The mystery that 'til now thousands
of veils concealed, my soul told, with
grace.

The dervish who unveils the world's great

mystery,

every moment bestows on you... more than

royalty.

That is no real dervish who begs for bread,

it's that one who raises out from the dead,

immortality.

If you had in your power your soul for an
hour,
all the prophets know... you'll also be the
knower.
Hidden face sought through time, space,
your mind's eye in the end will know, will
discover.

O You, from the heavens, of recent

birth...

You brought heaven's mysteries to

earth.

All rejoice at Your thunderous voice:

roar heart's lion, tear my soul... it has

worth?

Tonight, my Beloved revealed to me a
mystery…
O blessed night, long life to you, let it
be!
Tonight black ravens with soul's white
falcon spread wings and soar together,
free!

Perfect, perfect, perfect: this love is three times
perfect...
empty, empty, empty: this flesh, of lust has no
defect.
Holy, holy, holy: this light's three times holy in
effect...
meeting, meeting, meeting: today it meets the
infinite!

NOTES
(signified with an asterisk *next to the word)

DERVISH... To Rumi and Hafiz, 'dervish' was the word they used to signify a spiritually sincere seeker or one who had attained Realisation. They preferred to be called a 'dervish,' rather than a 'sufi,' which often meant a ritualistic connection with a sect which had little to do with the essence of Sufism: the love of God, respect for all approaches to God and the belief in the need to have a Perfect Master to attain God-realisation.

WINEBRINGER... Sometimes when Rumi uses the word 'winebringer' /saki/ he means a waiter or waitress who serves the juice of the grape in the wine-house or tavern and at other times he means the *Qutub* or Perfect Master who serves the devotee or lover of God spiritual Wine (Truth, Love, Grace).

KHIZER... Khizer is often called: 'The Green One' for he was said to have drunk from the Fountain of Immortality and gained Eternal life. He has been identified with Elias, St. George, Phineas, the Angel Gabriel, the companion of Mohammed on a journey which is told in the *Koran,* viii, 59-81, and throughout the literature of Mysticism has appeared to many great seekers who eventually became Perfect Masters. Many commentators have been confused by his periodic appearances throughout history. They do not understand that one of the Perfect Masters or the Rasool or Avatar of the age (whatever age it is) has the function and ability (can unlock the 'office' of Khizer) to appear to anyone in need at any time or place in the form that he wishes to take. When an aspirant is without a Master or his or her Master has died (as in the case of Francis of Assisi), one of the Perfect Masters appears to the aspirant to guide him or her to a Perfect Master (as Attar did to Hafiz) or to help with a problem, or to give God-realisation (as in the case of Francis).

SOLOMON… The Perfect Master who had the ability to travel on the wind and also to understand the language of the birds.

KALANDAR… Kalandars are lovers of God who have given up attachment to desires and live only for God. The name comes from a Master named Kalandar Yusuf. The word means 'pure gold.' Kalandars are continually on the move and care nothing for their own condition, as they are only concerned with praising God. Hafiz says that the real meaning of kalandarship is scrupulous attention to detail and never giving in. In other words, the outer appearance doesn't matter and a true kalandar is inwardly meticulous in giving up all his desires to God. John the Baptist was probably a kalandar-type Perfect Master.

SUFI… The mystic of Islam. In the true sense of

Sufism (love of God, respect for the essence of all paths to God, the need for a Perfect Master to help one to attain unity with the Beloved) Rumi was a Sufi, a true Sufi. But Rumi recognised that any approach to God can become abused and many 'Sufis' at the time when he lived were doing this, and he continually criticised their hypocrisy and deceit.

NOAH... The Perfect Master, the God-conscious soul.

HALLAJ... The Perfect Master and martyr Mansur Hallaj (d.919 A.D.), who was sentenced to hang for saying: "I am the Truth (Anal Haq)." (In *ghazal* 217 couplet 6 *Divan of Hafiz,* my translation... see bibliography, Hafiz makes the same statement, which must have made it difficult for him from then on, if he made that poem public). Much has been written about Hallaj and his famous (and infamous) statement. If the reader wishes to follow up his life and writings, see: 'Muslim Saints and Mystics' by Farid ud-Din Attar trans. by A.J. Arberry R.K.P. pp. 264-272; 'The Kashf al-Mahjub: The Oldest Persian Treatise on Sufism' by Hujwiri. trans. by R.A. Nicholson, Luzac, U.K. ' Hallaj: Mystic & Martyr' Louis Massignon, Princeton University Press 1994. For his poems see my 'Mansur Hallaj: Selected Poetry, New Humanity Books, 2012.

RAMADAN, KORAN NIGHT... Ramadan is the ninth month of the Muslim year, during which there is a daily fast. The *Koran* manifested to Prophet Mohammed during this month and this is called 'The Night of Power' or 'The Koran Night'- but the exact day that this falls on is not known.

KAABA... The holy shrine at Mecca to which Muslims pray and make pilgrimage to.

MOUNT SINAI... The mountain on which Moses saw God in the form of Divine Light, i.e.: the burning bush.

JESUS... In Persian Poetry the breath of Jesus (The Messiah) restores life. Here Rumi's Master (Shams –e Tabriz) is likened to Jesus.

REND... According to Steingass' *Persian-English Dictionary* 'rend' means: 'sagacious, shrewd; a knave, rogue; a Sufi; dissolute; a drunkard, debauchee; one whose exterior is liable to censure, but who at heart is sound; a wanderer, traveller; and insolent, reckless, fear-nought fellow.' The image of the *rend* is deeply rooted in the early medieval social and cultural history of Central Asia and Iran.

STAR... The Prophet Mohammed whom this poem praises..